Honeycomb

KRITHIKA SHRINIVAS

Copyright © 2012 Author Name

All rights reserved.

ISBN-13: 978-0692177433 (Krithika Shrinivas)
ISBN-10: 0692177434

DEDICATION

dedicated to all the dreamers of the world. i hope you never stop pushing your boundaries.

CONTENTS

amber (part i) 3
april 4
arson 5
color 6
if i was a song 9
gardening 11
dreams 12
flower crown 13
random musings 14
never again 15
incomplete 16
february 17
growing up 18
childhood 20
adulthood 23
healed 24
our own ways 25
assumptions 28
a little too much 30
to those hurting 31
hold on 33

moonless night	34
clichés	35
kites	38
immigrants	39
adolescent lullaby	40
hope	43
orange	44
belonging	47
uneducated	48
scared men	50
stranger in a coffee shop	51
secrets	53
history	55
ignorance	58
little dandelion	60
making love with music	63
alone	65
light and love: a physics lesson	66
reconnecting	69
the voice mail	72
mirror	75
cookie	77
winter renewal	80

carnival love	82
nature's warriors	89
this is goodbye	90
unhealthy diets	92
confessions of a claustrophobe	93
an ode to aphrodite	94
frosted hearts	95
winding lanes: the pilot	97
poem (noun)	99
work in progress	100
amber (part ii)	103

ACKNOWLEDGMENTS

to my parents for being my rock and helping me take the thoughts i've held onto for so long and pour them onto paper. i am eternally grateful for your support.

to my brothers, kaushik and cocoa. although one of you is furry and the other one not so much, thank you both for being here for me.

to my teachers, mr. wisniewksi, mr. carrillo, and mr. martinak for believing in me throughout my academic journey and paving my way to success. thank you.

to my guidance counselor, mr. glassberg, for being my pillar of support and bringing out the best in me. i couldn't have made it this far without you.

to my friends- you know who you are. thank you for the best memories, love, and encouragement. i'm so grateful to have such beautiful people in my life.

to my friends from the iowa young writers studio for helping me become a better writer and person. i wish we could have another two weeks in our favorite city.

and to you, my reader, for supporting me as a writer by purchasing this book. thank you for believing in me and what i have to offer.

amber (part i)

please freeze these vowels

let them shimmer in gold hues;

immortalize me.

april

crumbled butter cookie dust that clings to grey sweatshirts

cream soda that melts on winter-numbed tongues

grey skies that part for bluer hues

leather bound books that are laced in pollen

cocoon eyes that finally flutter

trees that fall in love again

arson

do not douse your fires

because the world is too scared to burn.

instead,

show them what is truly light.

color

life is not black and white-

some days can be burgundy,

fall leaves crunching beneath sodden boots,

hot cocoa sipped by a crackling fireplace,

mucus layered noses,

and lipstick that paints faces like a canvas.

some days can be grey,

Honeycomb

when the news drones on the television,

stale dinner sits at the counter,

hair is half dry, half frayed with raindrops,

and the wind roars angrily outside.

some days can even be yellow,

sunlight surging on wilting faces,

sipping lemon tea with dew drop eyes

birds waltzing about in the clear sky

as children dance in circles.

of course there are days of red

when hearts pour out venom

and days of blue when

the stars sing us lullabies,

and days of fuchsia,

when cheeks are tinted in brilliant hues

and heads spin

and nails dance along wooden desks

and vinyl records are scratched into music.

-for every moment is teeming with color.

if i was a song

if i was a song, i would spill out of cracked lips, blood seeping through jagged, papery skin like a jigsaw puzzle, only to coat my lyrics. my melody would glide like water from a golden chalice, hugged by grace notes and gentle chords, as if it's scared to break through. my harmony would resonate softly in the background, coiling around eardrums like a base clef, yearning to be appreciated. if i was a song, i'd start off soothingly. i'd shut the eyes of the weary with the angelic notes of a soprano, the rhythm steady, repetitive, even, so much so that the lyrics collide together past recognition. i would comfort you before i mourned to myself. the notes would steep downward, an abrupt pause ensuing before they curve off the edge of the page, the tonality grumbling. the flats are scattered, whimpering out jarring, overlapping cries as finger pads press on them. the keys groan in agitation as the lyrics grow painful, frustration dripping off of aching gums. the piano hammers jolt in anguish, bouncing with every forlorn stroke as my lyrics tumble in their rawest form- confused, broken, lost, irate. the words burst, fragments amplified by the melodramatic pedal that longs to spread the loneliness past its metal confines. and then i would stop. the anger would diminish out of my melody. i'd ease into a startling quietness

Honeycomb

and the listeners will start to bob their heads again like rocking chairs. the sharps would quiver with melancholy notes as i grow dark and tragic, drizzling off of keyboards, fluid arias into the air. and then i would end, fingers lingering on keys and lyrics melting into a final, wavering note that borders on hopeful but also so beautifully hopeless.

gardening

never stop picking out the weeds in your garden.

soon, flowers will decorate every shrub.

do not let these weeds suffocate you.

dreams

do not throw away your dreams. if anything, bury them and water them so the next generation can pluck the petals of your forsaken ambition and scatter them across the world. whatever you do, do not waste them. allow them to thrive in any way possible, even if that can only be as a seed.

flower crown

her flower crown falls,

smeared against the asphalt,

blood of pink and yellow,

flattened, dry veins.

her hair is left awry.

random musings

when you are left with nothing,

but a pair of eyes to filter in the horizon,

paint yourself the life you wanted

between mountain silhouettes,

patches of clouds,

and worn-down sunsets,

with the ink that stains your fingers.

never again

Before you leave me,

hand me the spare silver key

and I'll lock my heart.

incomplete

when my heart broke,

it was covered in cracks,

bloody and raw.

i needed flesh

to fill the holes

that had left me so empty,

so i took your skin

and draped it over the gaps.

i was just trying to fill the space.

[i'm sorry i didn't love you enough]

february

we sip on chamomile tea, crushed petals pooling on our tongues.

quilts are strewn across marble kitchen floors-

hiding earthly silhouettes.

our tongues are glazed in dark chocolate,

layered in hearty bourbon.

amid the sludge, sturdy bark blushes,

stripped by zealous wind.

growing up

the water turned red and blue and green, mingling with finger paints inside the laundry room sink.

the kitchen floor groaned as mud imprinted its surface, just after a soapy scrub-

now it knows of nothing but sparkling tile.

the moldy attic stairs ache to feel contact with flesh, hear the screeches of moving suitcases, and resonating laughter growing distant.

the chandelier sobbed when it met the tennis ball one rainy evening-

it can't complain anymore because no one even flicks the switch on.

the armchair by the window yelped as nails dug into its fabric-

Honeycomb

these days it watches the dew drops kissing the elm tree alone,

yearning for a human body to hold it close.

the doorbell whimpered, glancing every now and then at the obstinate door

…sealed firmly at its hinges.

come back, little girl

come home and play with us

childhood

Their eyes gleam of glistening stars,

bursting colors projected through their irises,

streaked with imagination.

And while age must dull their vivid thought,

for now they are unrestrained,

their brains untampered,

unhindered by mankind's *civility*.

They are suffused in controversy and excitement and ideology

that grown adults cower to make heard,

Honeycomb

Past their sewn, rigid lips.

The child knows of sodden earth and mud stained pants,

sweet peach trees and chilly air, dancing across the mountaintop.

Their knees are scraped from adventure's touch, their hearts of shimmering

gold;

with sweaty palms entangled, they gallop about, silhouettes that stain the

horizon.

Their minds are lit with candlesticks,

so much so that they fear the dark.

But their worries never last long enough,

cured by a wandering mind and a mother's touch.

Soon their eyes darken into voids,

stars rattled- shaken away by bleak asteroids.

Honeycomb

The light of their minds crackle and fizz,

an omnipresent darkness reigning their thoughts.

The infant once dipped in holy water

is bathed in sin and greed,

a raging sense of destruction that grows only with age.

Their smiling lips are hardened,

drooping constantly under the weight of their sorrow.

And once their burdens cling far too deep into the rungs of their spine

as they shuffle, clumsily in their misery;

And once their eyes cannot see past the shadow of their thought,

blinded by their vanity,

They dance across the mountaintop.

Sweaty palms entangled, they gallop about,

silhouettes that stain the horizon.

adulthood

So this is growing up

Counting tax returns instead of stars

Draining wallets, not crayon boxes

Climbing corporate ladders, not picket fences

We run to interviews instead of candy stores,

Making promises we cannot keep

(at least not with pinky promises)

We have thrown away our orange juice,

Filling up the cartons with bitter coffee and stale ciders

(there's no more nap-time, after all)

Our palms crave for the chalk powder silhouettes,

That we have replaced with ink and tears

We don't play in the mud anymore;

We've gotten our hands dirty enough now anyway

healed

You know you are healed

when the thing that causes you pain

and the thing that relieves you

are two separate things.

our own ways

everyday,

the ocean kisses the sand-

mellowly-

before retreating back into its glory.

they never hold each other,

mixing into sludge.

everyday,

the sunset cradles the horizon,

embracing her in pink and orange,

telling her that she's more than the blue

that meets people's eyes.

but when the time comes,

she slithers away,

Honeycomb

instead of blanketing her hues

across the lonely sky.

everyday,

the wind rustles leaves,

watching as they gently brush each other,

their stems shaking.

it's never for too long,

because when it leaves,

the leaves are alone- motionless,

still, longing.

every night,

the sun lets the moon shine,

enabling her with radiance.

for a few hours,

the moon is overjoyed,

Honeycomb

illuminating the pavement

before the sun takes back this gift.

everyday,

i see you.

we say hello, how are you, goodbye,

words seared on our tongues from overuse.

you are warm and kind,

your eyes lit with a passionate fury

that your smile subdues.

and before long,

you are on your own way

as i am on mine.

you will always be out of reach.

assumptions

you do not know,

the ancestry that clasps

to the rungs of my spine

like metal fishing hooks,

nor can you see the tinges

that flicker through my eyes-

those of forefathers

who can no longer sit by you

Honeycomb

and tell you of my story.

you see the version of me

that my sculpted cheekbones

and carved eyes tell you to see

but i can see every gene

that was unable to stand the test of time.

so don't tell me who i am.

a little too much

i dream too much, i hope too much, and i think too much. i do everything a little too much because sometimes you have to do a little too much to have a little too much.

in the space here, make a list of all your dreams

to those hurting

when you're sad,

wisps of your hair clinging to the crinkles of your pillow,

your lips stained with mother's cocoa-

look at the pregnant clouds,

their bodies arching as they tear apart,

bursting into showers.

watch as the lightning cuts through the fog,

although the thunder frightens it,

with its irate bellow.

it lacerates the air,

hot fire that steams rain droplets,

choking out promises

that the storm will end-

one stroke at a time.

do drink another sip of your cocoa.

hold on

it's okay to not have everything figured out.

it must've taken the moon a while

to realize how brightly she could shine too.

moonless night

the man on the moon strokes his pudgy palms onto the surface of his home, the ash clouding his crescent-nailed fingers. his weary body nestles against a pointed star, stitched on velvet cloth, his hand clutching chalk dust that leaves the night dark.

silhouettes clump together, amorphous ballerinas that waltz across the cracks of jagged pavements. their sharp eyes are illuminated by dusky streetlights that stain their pupils yellow.

the stormy wave parts like cracked lips. her foamy figure renounces its attack on the plateaued rock, the conch resonating her stillness. she ceases her fluid dance, a glutinous pool that drowns childrens' reflections.

when the wolf howls, it is astray in its gaze.

clichés

beauty does not come from the inside,

for if that was the case,

Mother Teresa would've been a super model-

her eyes glowing in a vanity her heart has never known.

nor is it in the eye of the beholder,

for i have come to know

that most beholders are blind.

it is only fair that we cry over spilled milk.

if we do not, dairy farmers will lose their jobs,

and we'll all become lactose intolerant-

eventually.

if i could be myself,

i would be a water bamboo,

nestled cozily in a corner,

hidden from sunlight-

and people.

love is blind, they tell me,

their fingers flicking across Tinder

as they swipe left,

over and over again.

if actions speak louder than words,

let's just stop talking

and lead life like it's a silent movie.

absence makes the heart grow *needier*,

Honeycomb

struck by desperation and anger,

confusion and ache.

perhaps it will forget of love altogether.

surely altitude is determined by attitude,

if most people's altitudes were crushed sandcastles.

this poem may not be as good as gold

but i don't care

as long as you are as happy as a clam.

kites

When the wind scatters the clouds,

leaving the sky sewn in melancholy,

kites fly,

their greens and reds and blues

gliding through the grey.

They have never seen sunlight;

heat leaves them motionless,

rendering them incapable.

When faced by adversity,

we rise to our greatest heights.

immigrants

My parents came to America with 60 dollars,

clutched between their anxious fingers-

the same ones they used to build me my future.

So when you tell me to go back to my country,

I gaze at the beige walls of my house,

built atop their weary bones,

looking at the ceiling as they have,

sleepless in their ambitions.

I stand still.

adolescent lullaby

rest your head, my little dearie,

against the crook of my neck,

for one day it will know of

plastered car seats,

darkened alleyways,

and cold beds that bruise your head.

gurgle on your milk, sweet child,

let it draw your eyes shut,

Honeycomb

like our sheer curtains,

before your lips are traced in purple,

the way your father's were.

when your pupils roam the dark,

count sheep in your head, my love,

instead of the crimson dashes

they will etch on your skin one day,

chiseling you into their artwork.

dream a little dream, my angel,

of sunlit meadows,

where your toes dust the earth.

the flowers will dance in greeting,

as you look to the sky,

and the clouds will part for you.

Honeycomb

in the morning, my baby,

i will kiss your stray hair,

gently rocking your limp body,

as you wake up.

you must always wake up.

hope

there will come a day

when the sun folds onto the earth

and the asphalt drips of gold

and violets sleep on mountaintops

and smiles are drawn in strawberries

and not etched by knives

and when we dip our brushes in the sky

we can create watercolor paintings

and not charcoal smears from smoke

that has filled our lungs for too long

and that is the day

we will be happy.

orange

i have been hidden—

under the weight of orange rinds.

they hold my naked feelings,

a new mother holding her infant

to the warmth of her chest.

my thoughts diffuse

around a compressed membrane-

seeping through cracks in hunger.

coiling in on themselves,

they watch the darkness of their shell

like an eclipse that threatens the sky.

you are hesitant in your touch,

Honeycomb

but your fingers roll across the pores,

my surface softening with your oils.

your fingernails are caked in skin,

white folds and orange crescent moons.

you place it all to the side,

skin and barriers and peels alike,

scooping flesh out of your nails,

like pumpkin seeds.

you do not throw away my protection—

that which was once a part of me.

in your hands,

my mind is naked,

eyes spinning like fan blades as

Honeycomb

i cling to the flesh i don't have.

you can see it all.

i let you squeeze my thoughts

onto the rugged palm of your hand.

your wrists are perfumed in citrus

with whispers of musings-

lemon trees, gardens, and love somewhere in the middle.

you pour it all into a glass

so my feelings char your throat-

the farthest they've been from me.

you make incense with the rinds on your counter,

freeing me at last.

belonging

i can't tell you when was the first time i felt alone,

but i can tell you the way my face stung with heat

and the thoughts that my brain swallowed

with a crumbling smile;

i faltered words that didn't belong

with a presence that didn't belong either.

i can also tell you that there never will be a last time.

uneducated

don't spill your honeyed words into my ears,

for my mother has raised me on lullabies

too pure for your hungry, cracked lips to fathom.

she has taught me of weeping willows and moonlit nights

while you've taught me of watery eyes and crestfallen faces.

don't hold me on a subway for everyone to see

the way your hands press on flesh

that isn't marked with the spiraling arches

of your looming finger pads.

don't paint these barren nights

in red from bottles that ache for you

in a way i can no longer.

Honeycomb

i came to you for love

but only experience can teach somethings.

scared men

Sorry that you have to look at her the way you do-

She is radiant in her beauty,

Almond eyes and cream skin,

Raven hair planted by the night sky itself.

When she stands tall,

you shrink.

Just don't expect her to shrink to the level of your manliness.

stranger in a coffee shop

we could've sipped peppermint tea

on a ragged couch patched up

with old memories filling the seams,

air spun with cinnamon sugar and vanilla,

like melted cotton candy.

we could've played old piano melodies,

fingers dusting the ivory keys,

lined in lint and harmonies

that have left the board yellowed.

we could've grilled corn on the barbeque,

the smoke scaring away the clear air

that drifted from the mountains

Honeycomb

and onto our gleaming faces

as the purple sky erupted in your eyes.

we could've read poetry together,

buried under wool blankets

with your warm breath in my ear,

laced in cappuccino and sleepiness

as your eyes droop with every stanza.

but you shove the receipt in your pocket,

smoothing your dark hair away

from the creases that rest near your eyes,

the bells of the door chiming as you walk away.

your half drank espresso lies on the table,

cold and bitter.

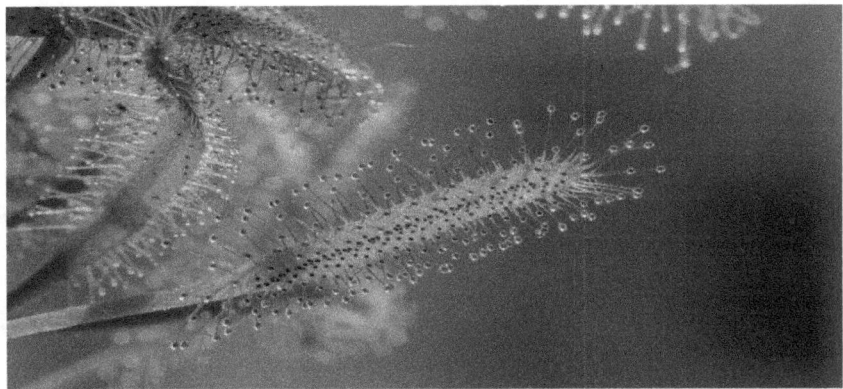

secrets

Reigning castles in the air,

Whispers justifying their flair,

Stained cheeks and memories,

Haunted souls and felonies,

Grudgingly played melodies,

Irately written obituaries,

Marked wrists and untold tales,

Limp bodies that lie so frail,

Warped words in sewn quilts,

Honeycomb

Codes strewn, like common silt,

Seances and speeches left unspoken,

Broken mirrors and carnival tokens,

Hair left awry- untamed,

Demise disintegrates ghastly blame,

Locked up in hearts were all that dark and cold,

The killer of all were mysterious untold.

history

in wilted pages of crinkled petals,

violet blood oozes-

written word,

that once stained the skulls of decapitated rulers.

the love-struck queen and the masochist king-

how they are glorified,

by the pointed pen that taints their surface,

their blood spilling across paper

like the plague that filled the streets they died in.

jubilant balls of frilly dressed maidens,

dye painted eyes,

cranberry smeared lips,

glistening goblets lit under chandelier kisses,

Honeycomb

roasted duck with crinkled skin,

the princess waltzes,

her auburn hair is streaked in mosaics,

dark blue, forest green, dirty yellow.

the drawbridge is reeled like a fishing hook,

night tainting the faces of visitors

who meld into shadowy silhouettes-

and though ink does not capture their color,

they are all immortalized,

those at the ball that night.

and like them,

drape me across the layered sheets-

stretching my skin past their bony confines-

interweaving flesh and paper.

dot me in ink and grab my silenced stories;

Honeycomb

i have hid them between my teeth,

coated atop every murmur.

make me the princess i was not born to be.

write of me as if my fingers know not of calluses-

my eyes are free of weariness-

my body is unaware of longing.

make me dance at the ball,

footprints marking the marble.

make me die of the plague,

instead of this ordinary heartbreak.

i have spilt my blood to make a name for myself.

make me history.

ignorance

Words are meaningless

To those who don't turn an ear

Scattered beams of language

Are not what they hold dear

We can't show eloquent lines

To those who refuse to read

We cannot show love

To those who practice greed

Poetry is for the broken

But not the realist

How can you understand pain

When you impose a fist

Honeycomb

No matter what you do

No matter what you try

The blind cannot see your pain

And the deaf cannot hear you cry

little dandelion

The apple doesn't fall far from the tree

Maybe I'm not the apple then.

Perhaps I don't even hang from a tree—

I am my own entity,

A dandelion.

My mother holds my dainty stem,

Her fingertips leaving dented bruises on the green tube.

She blows my wisps away;

Honeycomb

I disperse into oblivion,

my flowers falling on the golden ringlets of a young girl,

compressing on the asphalt as they roll along a bike tire,

floating gracefully toward the clouds,

ballerinas shuffling their tutus,

waiting to camouflage with an entity bigger than themselves.

The apple doesn't fall far from the tree

Maybe I'm not the apple then.

Perhaps I don't even hang from a tree—

I am my own entity,

A dandelion.

With every raspy breath on me,

the gasp of air with every scream,

I drift away,

escaping knotty fingers and mud stained earth.

Honeycomb

my skin is not bruised with my fall;

I do not stare glumly above,

at the fruit that hangs low—

trembling with every winter chill—

waiting to suffer a similar fate

[blow me away from all that I have known]

making love with music

the crook of your elbow fits

snugly against the wooden curve

of my cello body.

resin marks linger

across my sturdy frame;

you dot me in your dusty notes.

metallic knobs shiver,

twisted by nimble fingers;

Honeycomb

my music whimpers in cacophony.

a flat, b sharp, c minor

strings jolt in fervor,

plucked by gentle flicks;

staccato gasps echo in your ear.

rest two, three, four

your bow glides across the frets,

harmonies melding with the air,

as you take in my melody.

crescendo e diminuendo

Crescendo: a musical notation suggesting a gradual increase in loudness

Diminuendo: a musical notation suggesting a gradual decrease in loudness

alone

my lovers are whispered melodies

that glide into my eardrums,

hollowed without the sound of voices.

i am held together by these bed sheets

that stitch me into their seams

like a child they pity.

sometimes if i get lucky,

the looming darkness kisses me goodnight.

light and love: a physics lesson

sometimes when i'm sad,

you sing rainbow love songs to me,

hoping that the beams of color collide in my ears,

roygbiv.

visible light[1].

you send shooting stars through my lips

streaming in light with every breath;

it dances on my tongue--

a splattered comet.

refraction[2].

your hues illuminate my mirror,

Creeping through the edges of the glass.

Honeycomb

my irises glow.

my veins flow with your gold.

my neck shimmers with your sunlight.

dispersion³.

on some days,

broken lightning pours out of your wrists.

your tongue is coated in fog as you speak:

stormily, self-deprecatingly.

my golden eyes beg to differ.

doppler's effect⁴.

as the sun eclipses,

you pack away your colors.

my eyes burn into ash,

my lips crack,

a shattered prism.

r..0..y..g..b..i..v..

an absence of light[5].

Visible light: all colors of a rainbow mixed together forms visible light

Refraction: the bending of light from one medium to another

Dispersion: a beam of light is spread consequent to passing across an edge

Doppler's effect: wave energy changes relative to position of the observer

Absence of light: all colors of the rainbow are absent

reconnecting

your kisses travel in cosine waves,

my phone smugly receiving the love

that my hungry lips crave for.

i send one across the atlantic,

with a frequency of ∞,

when all of a sudden...

you/ are/ bre/aking/up/

i/wa/nt/to/hear/your/voice—

speak/fast/er/my/love

if/the/mol/ec/ules

of/that/beau/ti/ful voice

vi/brate/fast/er

the/sound/waves/

Honeycomb

trav/el/quick/er

and/you/can/fill/

my/ear/drums.

your static breath jumps,

leaping off of metal rods,

before tracing my ear

like a used handkerchief,

grazed by many mouths.

meters are measured in fingertips,

glazed across a crumbled map,

terrains and oceans stained,

in melted crimson lipstick.

sixteen thousand hugs-

ten thousand kisses-

Honeycomb

three thousand tears-

one barrier.

[call reconnecting…]

when the connection returns,

you tell me that you love me.

the voice mail

Hello and good day. I cannot answer the phone at the moment. For that matter, I can never answer the phone again. I left it back in 2018 since it kept annoying me.

Please send me a postcard instead. Or even better, a heartfelt letter. I want to see your handwriting— your sloppy cursive or your even print, the smudges of ink that branch off the corners of the page. I want to picture you reaching out to your coffee mug filled with pens and taking out an old black, gel pen, letting blots of black ink dot the page lightly before you pen the words, a slant to the left evident with the curvature of the letters and a slight gap between each letter, as if you were quivering when you wrote— perhaps you were nervous? afraid? frightened? merely upset? I have seen you communicate with me in the handwriting of a robot for years on end, staring between every double-spaced, Times New Roman, 12 pt line, trying to find the meaning between every letter. I can't tell if you were smiling or crying as you culminate your note with a yellow smiley face emoji that looks nothing like you. Please. Just stop hiding.

You shoot me a text at midnight on a Tuesday night and I find myself shoving my phone away because I'm tired. Tired of the generic "hey", "what's up", "you up?", "wanna chat?". But I find myself pacing down the stairs with the wind mangled in my hair as I rush out the front door when I see the USPS van approach the window. Because when you're given one page, front and back, you tell me what you have to. You tell me the truth. You tell me of how you woke up one morning and the scent of cherry blossom trees wafted into your bedroom and how you just felt the need to write about how ephemeral life is; how everything invariably withers into a black nothingness. You tell me of how you walked into a bookstore and the lady who was running it had hair as dark and straight as the shelves there and how she reminded you of your freshman year English teacher and how you miss high school all of a sudden. The truth is, when you're given one page, you're honest. You understand boundaries. You value human connection. But that changes when you're given 64 gigabytes and a plethora of emojis and a camera roll that defines your existence. You don't want to talk anymore. You just want to fill the space.

Honeycomb

We value instantaneousness. We value a quick response to our speedily typed paragraphs and find ourselves annoyed when we receive anything short of an empty reaction. Somehow we've mistaken instant gratification for depth, for whatever reason. Because when I hold a letter close to my face I can whiff out the scent of vanilla at the edges and coffee between each word as you place your coffee mug down, take a sip, and graze the page with your fingers. I can hear your laugh ring through the page with a few words and I can feel your ink mourn as the words get airier towards the end of the note as if you're mourning yourself. That this is all you can say to me for a few days. That you're going to miss me.

Please leave a message after the tone.

I can't promise that I will answer.

mirror

the bathroom mirror squeaks,

my towel running across its foggy surface.

the mist seems to resurface,

almost instantaneously,

until i rub the palms of my hand against the glass,

sweeping away the obscurity

my face pours into the screen,

skin stretching between the borders of the frame.

my eyes are bloodshot,

Honeycomb

pores speckled across my face—

streaked with hair,

dotted with acne,

the map of an unseen constellation

the light streams into her eyes-

azure-

smearing onto the mirror's canvas.

sloped nose of a curved trail,

oh this sculpted face-

carved lips of rose,

cheeks of oasis sand.

i scrub and scrub at the mirror.

my eyes remain brown.

dirty.

cookie

at the end of the day,

we can all classify ourselves as cookies.

we are born from cracked eggs and a stick of butter-

whisked to existence in a porcelain bowl.

a delicate hand drizzles baking soda over the batter that is us-

we are given the power to *rise*,

enveloped by the restorative love of our maker

before we meet our fate in the cozy oven.

we succumb to the heat,

the scorching sun melding with our being-

infiltrating our body, our soul-

and yet we rise with such adversity.

Honeycomb

we are cookies;

our batter is coated generously in granulated sugar-

pleasure, reward, hope

and yet we are speckled with salt-

merging flavors that create a wholesome product.

often we are the subject of multiple facades-

dotted in colorful sprinkles that veils our essence.

we are molded by society's precise hand,

our edges ripped away the blunt force of the cookie cutter.

our packaging defines us,

shimmery golden paper and pastel ribbons.

we are the face we uphold,

not the content that we possess.

Honeycomb

cast aside are those of us burnt and doughy,

our value lost amidst the wafting scent of the perfect holiday cookie.

we aren't made into a crumble or are we re-baked;

rather, we meet the trash can, sullen, lost, and speechless.

we are unsure of ourselves-

lost in tin cans and gauze bags and plastic boxes-

yearning for the acceptance of our beloved consumer.

they sink their teeth into our surface, piercing through our smooth exterior-

our melted chocolate and cream filling ooze through our skin-

past our façade, our conduct, our grace.

we are vulnerable at the mercy of the world.

[preheat to 325 degrees to produce a human being]

winter renewal

I find myself thawing at the ice on my car window one winter morning,

my bare fingers scraping against the rock, my nails tearing with the jarring impact—

jagged.

broken.

shattered.

And yet with bleeding cuticles I find myself going, ripping apart at the solid, waiting to see my ghastly reflection,

Staring back at me.

Honeycomb

I find myself thawing at the ice on my heart one winter morning,

my bare fingers cutting into the skin, my nails caked in maroon blood,

accompanying flesh holding it down.

jagged.

broken.

shattered.

And with bleeding cuticles I find myself going, ripping apart at the solid,

trying to rid myself of you,

The ice that has held you together for far too long.

carnival love

you gave me an extra [ticket] when i lost my own.

i WON two TEDDY BEARS at the 0 → toss.

and gave you one on your way →**out**

the next time I saw you

your syllables were s-e-w-n- in- c-o-t-t-o-n-c-a-n-d-y

so you stammered

with

a c r o s s y o u r c h e e k s

that glowed warmly

your hands rolled with mine,

Honeycomb

like saltwatertaffy.

gelato seeped through our tongues

before

   our

   screams

     B

     O

      U

     N

      C

     E

      D

    off

    the

    free

    fall.

Honeycomb

you bury me,

p l

    s t i

        c

  b a

    l l s

|-----against-----|

my lungs,

heldinplacebyyourWEIGHT

my/laughter/is/dismissed/as/yours/f i l l s/ my lips

our silhouette bodies hug the |walls| of the bouncy house.

you are *gentle*.

your breath wavers,

the quiet r|h|y|t|h|m of a

Honeycomb

```
        p   p   p

          e   e   e

        n   n   n

      d   d   d

    u   u   u

  l   l   l

    a   a   a

  m     m     m
```

like the r→ i → d → e → →

c   g

r   n   a **frightened** newborn

  a d l i

curing the a/pp///r////h-e-n///sive heart,

u/ne/ven in its b-e-a-t-s

and in its thoughts.

Honeycomb

when [you hold me],

your fingers smell of

popcorn p p o p r n

o p c op   o c   o p op co rn

o c c r n p n   op   c r o   n

p c o r no p c o or n

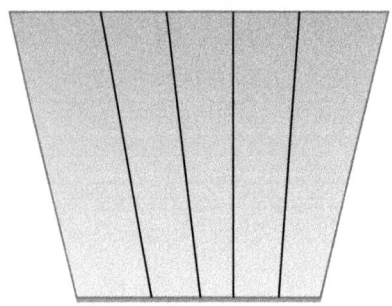

Honeycomb

greased in butter

and

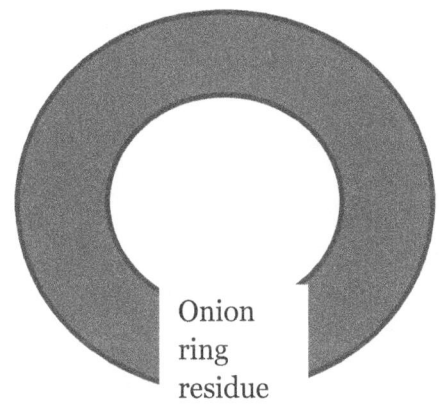

Onion
ring
residue

you smile like the merry circus clown,

and i want to take in your laughter

//like the ♪ ♪ music ♪ ♪ that keeps this tent together\\

Honeycomb

i find us going in circles

→ nowadays 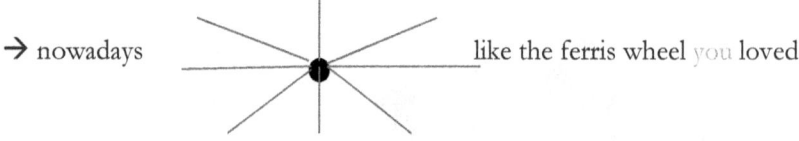 like the ferris wheel you loved

i want this ride to end.

nature's warriors

pooling below my sodden toes,

droplets

    tumbled

        toward

            the

                earth.

blemished ground,

painted in cloud blood.

mighty cumulonimbus has lost-

his wisps shrivel into stars.

    moonlight

        embraces

            the

                joyous

                    land.

this is goodbye

when you decide to leave,

i will show you out

the way i have,

countless times before.

i will watch your feet

trail the wooden floor

for the last time

as you eye the photographs

that i must take down

with broken nails

cut by glass shards

that cover every frame.

i will stand on the first step,

not the last,

Honeycomb

of the porch,

watching your head bob

as you walk away.

unhealthy diets

i stabbed my fork into sadness

this Sunday afternoon

slicing a sliver with my silver knife;

it tasted like cherry pie,

coated in a saccharine sweetness,

bleeding dirty blood into my rotten mouth

the taste of a love that has gone stale.

i gulp my glass of water.

confessions of a claustrophobe

the door is locked. ten chipped nails, broken cuticles, and earth-shattering sobs later, it is still shut tight, clenched in the grasp of a viper's mouth. i cannot be here forever. my knuckles wince in pain, pounding the obstinate metal with my sores knuckles, streaked in deep violet flowers. let me out. i'm shoving my head against this door, thoughtlessly, wordlessly. memories are jumbling around, blurry fuzzy movie stills. then i see the light.

my heart is locked. ten heart-breaks, crippling photographs, and insecurities later, i still cannot find the keys. i'm holding it in my hands, shaking it at my sides, hoping that if i rattle hard enough, i will somehow burst apart. all the memories would be regurgitated, word vomit that i can dispose of. i'm clawing at my fleshy heart, wincing with every tear. let it out. make me whole again. i'm holding my arms out, tears clouding my stormy eyes, heartstrings aching. tugging. then i see the light.

an ode to aphrodite

light cradles your cheekbones

hollowed beams of sun through your eyes;

melted gold

a heart resting on embers

to set the world aflame with such glowing love.

frosted hearts

nature's hue of green rusts to dead brown,

her branches paralyzed by frosted snow shavings

torrents of aggressive winds skin her sturdy bark;

she is kissed with crystalline ice,

the roots of her grass painted auburn

the sky is drained of its magnificent azure,

smeared lightly instead in greys,

fleeting. evanescent.

it is five million snowflakes past eight o clock,

Honeycomb

and i find myself in a heap of blankets,

strewn across the marbled kitchen floor,

clenching frostbitten fingers that have embraced the winter for far too long.

I wrap my hands around a mug of strong espresso,

as if the searing liquid could remedy my frigid hands,

a frozen heart of molded icicles and snowflakes;

all i feel is nothingness.

winding lanes: the pilot

you hold my hand for the last time and i find myself involuntarily drawing circles along your scaly knuckles with my fingertips. "last time," i remark, inwardly begging for anything but confirmation. you answer, knowingly, "last time".

the feelings are still human, real, spread like silhouetted skeletons across old vintage photographs, laced through ragged family quilts

leave me. throw me aside like the rag doll i've become. pick at my button eyes so the days grow blurry, hack away at my raven hair. leave me hollowed until you're left with the shell of a body, the memories imbedded in my heart gone so you can no longer feel guilty. cut my veins apart and claw apart my smile. leave me, but just take my memories with you.

you make planes fly everyday and yet i hope that every faltering step i take reminds you of your failure to keep me afloat

seal shut the corridors. it's time to land. you look out at the horizon, making sure the trajectory is all right and all you can see is the world on fire.

emergency landing. looks like your guilt has locked the controls in their places and you're stuck in the air. yet i have already moved on, past your petty, earthly grip.

i'm a lonely soul and somehow you happen to be within my magnetic reach.

poem (noun)

the wailing of hollowed trees embraced by a broken wind

gloved fingers thawing the ice of a frosted car window

curdled chocolate milk that you find in a state of desperate hunger

the song of an electrocardiogram that your jolting legs dance to

lukewarm bath water that has padded your fingers in webs

an involuntary breath that is heaved before a stormy sob

the echo of children's laughter that will soon reverberate only in our minds

work in progress

when i write,

syllables ricochet off of walls—

splattered ink staining crumbled pages

like a hardwood floor smeared in blood,

coughed from cracked lips.

the metaphors cave in on each other,

a string of farfetched syllables

Honeycomb

crudely defining my fragmented thoughts—

love to me is painted eggshells and foamy cappuccinos

(a normal mind wouldn't know)

when i write,

my audience yawns out my similes,

cliche comparisons clinging to their breath.

broken hearts and lonely souls are getting old

(maybe i am too)

i vomit out words,

consonants scraping my esophagus.

the ink pools near the drain of the sink-

by the edges of frayed paper-

can't you see that i'm ill?

Honeycomb

i'm too frail to write,

the paper strangling my neck,

with every haiku.

my musings scathe the lips of *real* poets

—bitter and smoky—

charred coffee that seeps into taste buds.

perhaps i've made them ill as well.

they slurp my broken allusions,

phlegmy soup that drapes their throats.

they cough and they cough and they cough.

take my cough syrup,

i croak.

it's made of ink drops.

amber (part ii)

i have been frozen

under the weight of my words.

here is my story.

ABOUT THE AUTHOR

Krithika Shrinivas is a New Jersey based writer of contemporary poetry and began writing this manuscript while enrolled in her junior year of high school in 2017. Krithika has been recognized for her poetry at a national and international level. Her previous publishing credentials include poetry in contests and magazines. She has been a finalist in the National Colorism Healing Poetry Contest in the Youth Poetry Division and has written for magazines such as the Ireland based *HEBE*. She had also attended the prestigious Iowa Young Writers Studio. Creative expression plays a huge role in her life, so along with writing, she is also an avid painter and singer. She seeks to use words as a means of bridging people together to enjoy the collective experience that writing brings.

www.ingramcontent.com/pod-product-compliance
Lightning Source LLC
Chambersburg PA
CBHW061334040426
42444CB00011B/2909